IMAGES
of England

CASTLE BROMWICH
CASTLE VALE
AND SHARD END

Castle Bromwich church, 1900.

IMAGES
of England

CASTLE BROMWICH
CASTLE VALE
AND SHARD END

Compiled by
Peter Drake and Marian Baxter

TEMPUS

First published 2000
Copyright © Peter Drake and Marian Baxter, 2000

Tempus Publishing Limited
The Mill, Brimscombe Port,
Stroud, Gloucestershire, GL5 2QG

ISBN 0 7524 2096 8

Typesetting and origination by
Tempus Publishing Limited
Printed in Great Britain by
Midway Clark Printing, Wiltshire

'D' and 'B' Blocks at Castle Bromwich Airfield, c. 1943.

Contents

Acknowledgements

Our thanks go to the Local Studies and History Section of Birmingham Reference Library, for the use of their collection of photographs.

We would also like to thank the following: Mr J. Foulger, Mrs J.B. Healey, Mrs P.M. Williams who lent photographs included in this publication; special thanks to the staff at Castle Vale Library who not only let us use their photographs but also put up with my presence while I sorted and scanned the photographs and asked lots of difficult questions; the Over 50s Club at Castle Vale and the Shard End Local History Society who helped with background information and photographs; Geoff Bateson whose 'History of Castle Vale' was an invaluable source of information for the first section of this publication; Gordon Cashmore for background information on Castle Vale and finally thanks to Geoff Cashmore and Maureen Cashmore for proof-reading the text.

Farm House at Shard End, Castle Bromwich, 1910. This is where Abraham Thornton lived up until the time of his trial for the murder of Mary Ashford in 1817.

Introduction

The first reaction of most people to the idea of a photographic history book of C'astle Bromwich, Castle Vale and Shard End is undoubtedly one of surprise. After all two large municipal housing estates and a pretty but unremarkable village on the outskirts of Birmingham do not seem to make the most interesting subject for a book of this nature. Yet there can be few such comparable districts close to a city centre anywhere else in the country that have such a fascinating history. A famous murder possibly committed by a Shard End farmer in the early part of the nineteenth century; a major Boy Scout camp visited by scouts from all over the country in wooded land at Yorkswood on the fringes of Shard End; the only surviving example of a formal eighteenth-century garden in the British Isles in Castle Bromwich and the sites of the British Industries Fair, Birmingham's first aerodrome and the aircraft factory which turned out most of the nation's supply of Spitfire aircraft during the Second World War in Castle Vale, are evidence of a rich and varied history. It is the intention of the compilers of this book to unlock this history and to turn the initial surprise of those who glance at the book into a deeper appreciation of the area and its history.

It would be misleading to describe these three places merely as suburbs of Birmingham. Castle Bromwich village in particular, has never been part of the city and both Shard End and Castle Vale have always been on its outer fringes. The districts are grouped together on the north and eastern side of Birmingham and were, before the expansion of the city in 1931, administratively part of Warwickshire. To the north and east they look out to Coleshill and Solihull. It is fitting therefore that this collection of photos of the area has been mainly selected from the collections in the Central Library in Birmingham, the home of the Warwickshire Photographic Survey. The Survey, which was instituted at the end of the nineteenth century, is a marvellous testimony to the Victorian passion for the photographic medium as a way of recording contemporary events, people and buildings. The traditions of the Survey have been continued more recently by groups such as the Shard End Camera Club. Nearly all of the photos reproduced here are being published for the first time, but they and many other photos of the district are always available for consultation in the Local Studies section of the Central Library. Both Birmingham and Solihull libraries would welcome further donations of photographs of the district.

Although the three areas are located next to each other and share some common history and characteristics, they are still very distinctive and each has a proud history and tradition. Of the three districts, Castle Bromwich is the only one which was ever really a village. It has gradually grown into a dormitory suburb of Birmingham and Solihull, but without entirely losing its village character. Many of the village features still exist today, the splendid church, the estate and country home in the shape of Castle Bromwich Hall, and a number of attractive old houses and pubs. Photographs of all of these are included in this book, usually from images from a hundred or so years ago. These buildings, and the lifestyle that they represent, are an age away from more modern developments in Castle Bromwich. These photographs show the many changes that have taken place, the building-over and destruction of fine houses and farms, and the loss of Whateley Hall and Park Hall to housing estates and to roads are sad reminders of a distant age. The rural nature of the nineteenth-century village is shown in the entry for Castle Bromwich in the 1872 Kelly's Directory. The entry concludes: 'The principal landowners are the Earl of Bradford, who is Lord of the Manor... The soil is sand; subsoil gravel. The chief crops are wheat, oats and barley. The area is 2,701 acres; the population in 1861 was 613, and in 1871, it was 689'. The construction of the M6 and the collector road have further affected the ambience of Castle Bromwich. Along with the road building in the post-war years, Castle Bromwich has expanded hugely with new private and municipal housing estates. It may have lost some of its identity but enough remains to make Castle Bromwich an attractive residential district.

Divided from Castle Bromwich by the River Tame, the Fazeley Canal and the M6, Castle Vale is very different area. It is basically a 1970s housing estate. Once the pride of its architects and the Birmingham City councillors who commissioned it, it has since be reviled as one of the worst examples of large scale high-rise housing, the estate has survived to enter a fresh period of selective demolition and improvement outside the day- to-day management of Birmingham City Council. The most striking aspect of the area now is the almost complete absence of any signs of its varied history. When the estate was built to house the displaced residents of Birmingham's inner cities, as those areas were themselves redeveloped, Castle Vale's links to the past disappeared. Castle Vale throughout the first sixty years of the twentieth century paid host to visitors from all over the world, including royalty and statesmen. However the district at this point was known not as Castle Vale, but by its ancient name of Berwood, otherwise it tended to be included in Castle Bromwich. The visitors came to The British Industries Fair, the forerunner of the National Exhibition Centre, to Castle Bromwich airfield and to the aircraft factory alongside the airfield. For two weeks every year the British Industries Fair was the most visited attraction in the country. Visitors arrived by road, by plane, or by train alighting at the long since departed Castle Bromwich railway station. All of these major sites and buildings have vanished under the new Castle Vale housing estate and one purpose of this book is to celebrate a time when the area stood for more than the image of the ills of large scale housing redevelopment.

Shard End by contrast has less of a history. Before the post-war housing estates were built, the area is marked on maps as mainly farms and woodland interspersed with the occasional large house. Much of the land was owned by the Earl of Bradford. It was one of the farmers, Abraham Thornton, who went down in legal history in the 1820s, as the last person in England to offer to fight a duel to confirm his innocence of the murder of a local girl Mary Ashford. The woodland on the fringes of Shard End at Yorkswood was turned into the site of a major Boy Scout camp with scouts from all over the country arriving at Castle Bromwich station and then trekking the few miles to Yorkswood. As an old 'Scouter' remembered, 'The nearest transport was the Fox and Goose, so the lads would have to walk to the site. Pushing their trek carts filled with equipment. Coming from all over the city often it would take a journey of over two hours and many scouts remember the fields and farmland that they went through'. The scout camp, along with most of the farmhouses, was replaced by housing in the 1950s. Much of modern Shard End shows signs of outer city neglect, a predominantly elderly population, little retail development, few communal facilities and depressed housing. Yet there is a thriving local history group for whose help and pride in their area, the compilers would like to acknowledge in compiling this book.

The varied geography of the three areas has had a crucial influence on their separate development. The hills of Castle Bromwich, from which Birmingham city centre six miles away is clearly visible, have shaped its village character in the same way that the large plain of Castle Vale made it ideal for an aerodrome and later, when the planes had left, for a completely new housing development. In Shard End the housing had to be fitted in around the River Cole. While the geography remains constant what has changed over the last hundred years has been the topography of the area. The three districts were at one time at the edge of the great Arden forest which covered much of Warwickshire and which had such an influence on William Shakespeare. Describing the grounds of Park Hall in Castle Bromwich, the local nineteenth-century antiquarian Christopher Chattock wrote: 'The place could not be surpassed for natural beauty and romantic interest, studied with wild cherries, roses and honeysuckle. Park Hall woods were filled with gigantic oaks, beech, ash and firs which overhung and darkened the clear crystal water of the River Tame below.' Sadly much of this sylvan scenery had disappeared before being captured on film but the area has still enough fascination and unexpected history to warrant bringing it to a twenty-first century audience.

Peter Drake and Marian Baxter
July 2000

One
Pre-war Castle Vale

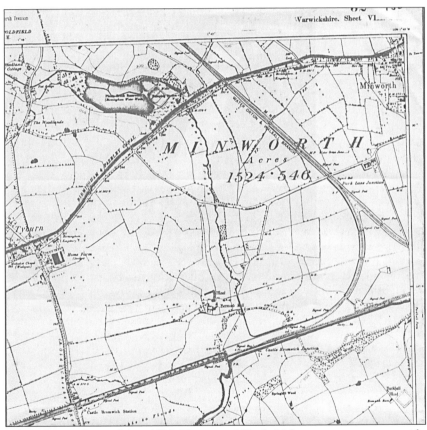

A six-inch Ordnance Survey Map, 1886. The area of Castle Vale was a very wet area with swamps and forests and was originally known as Berwood. A hermitage and messuage in the Manor of Berwood are mentioned around 1160, when the manor was given to the Cannons of Leicester Abbey. A chapel of Saint Mary at Berwood Hall is mentioned in the mid-thirteenth century, but was disued by the beginning of the fifteenth century when a survey lists the cannons' hall, a bakehouse, a dormitory, an oven, two barns, a cowshed and the old house beyond the precinct. The post-dissolution house, Berwood Hall, was also built outside of the moat, presumably on the site of, or incorporating, the old house or former agricultural buildings.

Berwood Farm. The six-inch Ordance Survey map of 1886, seen on the previous page, shows part of the moat with farm buildings and Berwood Hall to the south. No buildings are shown in the area which is enclosed by the moat, but stone foundations, thought to be those of Saint Mary's chapel, are said to have been visible in the 1920s. The buildings and the moat were removed and levelled for the construction of the airfield. In more recent years the site just off Farnborough Road, was occupied by Argosy, Comet and Lysander House. With the demolition of the high rise flats the area is awaiting the building of new homes in the year 2000.

Old farm buildings, Chester Road, 7 December 1931. Berwood derives its name from its early settlers. The Saxons, when settling in the valley of the heavily wooded area, called it 'Bearu,' meaning the woods. Over the years the meaning of the word was lost and when the next settlers arrived they gave their own meaning for woods, 'wulu'. The area then became known as BearuWulu. Thus, over the years, the low lying wet swamp and marsh valley, surrounded by the dense forests, became known as Berwood.

Old farm buildings, Chester Road, 10 December 1931. Home Farm stood on the Chester Road near to the Tyburn House. The Ordnance Survey maps of 1905 and 1921 show the farm and its orchard, but the 1938 map shows that the orchard had gone.

Old farm buildings, Chester Road, 7 December 1931. A *History of Castle Vale* by G. Bateson quotes, 'The Orchard had 650 tress all in straight lines on its 11 acres. On a good summers evening the branches were so heavy with fruit that they could be heard snapping. Farming a herd of dairy cows here had been so successful that in 1906 an electric milking machine was installed, enabling 14 cows to be milked at a time.' This must have been a novel innovation at that time.

A six-inch Ordnance Survey Map, 1905. As the housing in Birmingham rapidly expanded between the 1830s to the 1840s, the city was faced with the problem of what to do with its sewage. It was common practice at the time to collect the sewage in carts and dump it on water-logged land beyond the city boundaries for it to be dispersed by the rain. In 1881, William Walter Baggot sold 344 acres of the Berwood Farm land to the Birmingham Tame and Rea Drainage Board, followed by a further 358 acres in 1888. The sale of the Baggot land to the Drainage Board was to be a major factor in the formation of the flat land that was to become Castle Vale.

Plants Brook near Berwood, which ran through the centre of the area, and was diverted to the Minworth boundaries. The irrigation method of spreading sewage out over the surface of the land was an obvious one that needed ever increasing amounts of land as the amount of sewage to be treated increased.

Fields at Berwood. This left a large flat area for the sewage farming method to cultivate. Its production was to yield rich, large crops. The farm at one time was reported as being the best sewage farm in Europe. However, this method of farming could not continue indefinitely.

A steam plough at work on the sewage farm.

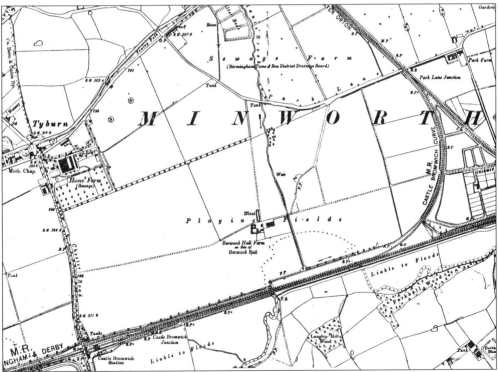
A six-inch Ordance Survey map, 1821. In 1898 the filtration method was introduced. The sewage was treated by passing it through filter beds. German prisoners and conscientious objectors constructed the compact filter beds. The new method of treatment also meant that much of the land could be sold off.

Castle Bromwich effluent channel.

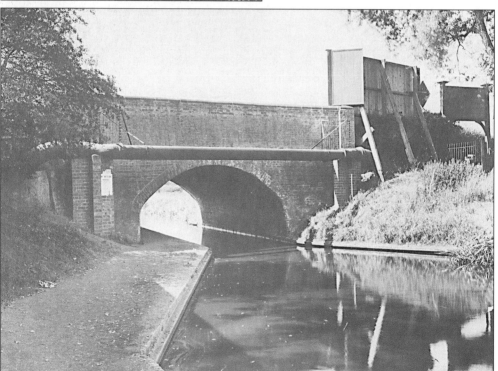

An Act of Parliament authorised the building of the Birmingham and Fazeley Canal in 1784, after a great deal of opposition from the well-established Birmingham Canal Company. Completed in 1790, the canal was built by John Smeaton.

Chester Road Canal Bridge, 3 March 1931. The next six photographs show the changes at the
Chester Road and Kingsbury Road junction over a period of roughly four years.

Chester Road and Kingsbury Road, 14 February 1934. The old road to Chester traces its existence back into antiquity and is probably the oldest road in the area. It traversed the empty wastes to join Watling Street at Brownhills. This was an important road as it was once the route taken by the Welsh drovers when they brought their herds to the markets of the Midlands and the South-East.

Chester Road looking across Kingsbury Road to the Canal Bridge, 22 October 1934. During the Scottish troubles in 1745, part of the Duke of Cumberland's army passed along this way on their march to meet the Pretender. Stopping off at the Bradford Arms at Castle Bromwich they sampled the local ale. The tale goes that the colonel left the pub without his sword, a fact that was not discovered until the group reached the Tyburn House, where they stopped to ask directions. The colonel was not therefore in the best of moods, and unfortunately the young man they asked for directions, was unable to answer because of a speech impediment. Angered by this and inflamed with drink the colonel ordered him shot as a spy. His head was cut off and, after throwing the body into a ditch, the head was carried to New Shipton Farm, in Walmley, where it was tossed into a tree. In 1827 the tree was felled and the skull discovered.

Chester Road and Kingsbury Road, 22 October 1934.

Chester Road and Kingsbury Road, 28 June 1935. The Chester Road became increasingly important for it was the main road to Chester, the port of embarkation for Ireland. In 1690 it saw the passage of over one hundred baggage wagons of provisions and troops sent by William III to his troops in Ireland.

Chester Road and Kingsbury Road, 28 June 1935. Saxton describes the Chester Road in his book *Bygone Erdington*, written in 1928, as: 'to our right as we leave the railway viaduct behind us we may discern the remnants of old Berwood Hall, now surrounded by the model farm buildings of the Sewage Farm, of which it now forms a portion. What a change indeed from the days when hereabouts were green pastures, still waters and the stately home of the mighty Ardens.'

Chester Road and Kingsbury Road.

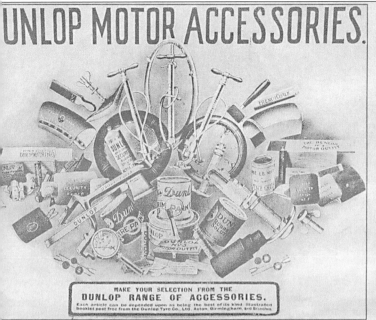

Early advertisements for Dunlop products. John Boyd Dunlop was a veterinary surgeon of Scottish origin who practised in Belfast. In 1888 he invented the first practical pneumatic tyre for his sons' tricycle. He and his six sons were to become the founders of the Dunlop Empire. John Dunlop resigned his directorship in 1895 and died in 1921, but his legacy was one of the greatest industries in the world. It has to be said that without Dunlop's invention the motor car would not have been possible because only pneumatic tyres could cope with the necessary power and cornering.

An aerial view of the Dunlop Works. The original company, the Pneumatic Tyre Company, became the Dunlop Rubber Company in 1900. It was established in Aston Cross, but by the outbreak of the First World War, demand far outweighed capacity. Work began on building Fort Dunlop in May 1915, when the 260 acre site at Castle Bromwich was purchased from Birmingham Corporation. Production began the following year. The workers had their own factory council, formed in 1919, and their dining room supplied between 4,000 and 5,000 meals a day. They had their own sports field of 27 acres with a sports pavilion and a fully equipped theatre in which they ran their own plays, dances and film society.

An aerial view of the Dunlop Works. It is said that Dunlop moved to England because the people of Dublin objected to the smell of rubber from the tyre factory and it was decided to relocate to the Midlands, which was the centre of the cycle industry. It is hard to think that the 260 acre site was originally a factory in the fields. The unusual name of Fort Dunlop seems to have come about because the factory was built during the First World War, when everyone was thinking in military terms. Another possibility for the name is that Fort Dunlop came from the mishearing of Port Dunlop, as it was a port on the canal.

Dunlop's test fleet of vehicles, c. 1928. In 1968, Dunlop was the ninth largest company in Britain. Its tyres, golf and tennis balls were known throughout the world. In recent years however, Dunlop and the markets failed. The ailing giant was taken over by British Thermoplastics and Rubber Industries in 1985, the tyre manufacturing section having already been sold in 1983 to the Japanese firm Sumitomo.

Car tyres being automatically sorted by size before inspection at Fort Dunlop. Over the years Dunlop has made tyres, latex yarn, semtex tiles and adhesive compounds. In the mid-1950s the range included Dunlopillo latex foam for furnishings, sports kits, golf and tennis balls, adhesives and even hot water bottles. In addition to its tyres it also manufactured wheels, brakes and electrical controls for cars, trucks and both civil and military aircraft.

Chester Road at the British Industries Fair entrance, 18 May 1931. Other early factories in the Berwood area were the Gunanogen Fertiliser Company (which reclaimed the treated sewage) and the Toro Soap Works. These, together with the glue factory and the sewage farm did not do much to enhance the atmosphere of the area!

Chester Road at the British Industries Fair entrance, 4 November 1931. The central rectangle of land, between Castle Bromwich, Minworth and Erdington, (which is now Castle Vale) remained empty, except for Home Farm and the semi-derelict Berwood Hall Farm.

Chester Road at the British Industries Fair entrance, 4 November 1931. In 1909, 250,000 acres of land was leased to the Housing and Open Spaces Association. In 1913 a further 33 acres was used by Birmingham Corporation Parks Department as a recreational ground. Up to 60 football matches could be played at one time on the marked out pitches. They provided welcome recreation for the local factory workers.

Chester Road at the British Industries Fair entrance, 13 February 1933.

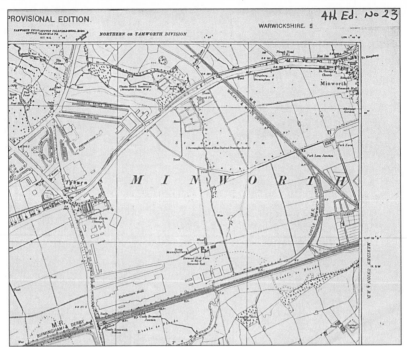

A six-inch Ordnance Survey Map, 1938. The 1938 map shows considerable changes from an earlier edition in 1921 (see p15). The orchard at Home Farm, shown on the 1921 map, had been built on. By 1938 the map shows the soap factory, on the site of Berwood Hall, and the British Industries Fair buildings. On the other side of Chester Road there are few buildings and the fields still border the road.

Chester Road and the British Industries Fair, 15 September 1937. In the 1920s the originators of the British Industries Fair successfully accomplished their goal of establishing a fair in the Midlands. The original nine and a half acres of ground rapidly expanded to provide halls in order to display exhibits of all kinds, which were seeking markets in every part of the world.

ON ARRIVAL AT THE FAIR

ADMISSION On presentation of a Trade or Official Announcement Card a Season Badge of Admission will be issued on payment of 2/6, Overseas buyers are admitted free of charge on presentation of their trade cards. The public are admitted on payment of 2/6 per visit after 2 p.m.

DURATION The Fair will be open from 9.30 a.m. to 6 p.m. each day from Monday, 6th May, to Friday, 17th May, when the Fair closes at 4 p.m. The Fair will not be open on Sunday, 12th May.

GROUPING The Fair is arranged in Groups according to Trade. Directional Signs at the Entrance and in the Gangways indicate very clearly where Groups and Stands are situated.

FACILITIES All the usual facilities, Post Office, Restaurants, Overseas Buyers' Club, Cloak Rooms for Hand Luggage, etc., are available within the Fair. Have your letters addressed to the BIF Enquiry Office, during the Fair, to be called for.

A visitor page from a British Industries Fair programme. Hangers, that had been used to house the planes used in the First World War, were utilised to house the British Industries Fair, an early forerunner of the National Exhibition Centre.

Birmingham Municipal Bank at the British Industries Fair, 1929. The fair was described as a place where buyers and sellers could meet, and where buyers could examine lines and commodities produced, not just by one, but by many manufacturers. Being a business fair there are no side shows or amusements, but every possible provision was made for the conveyance of visitors.

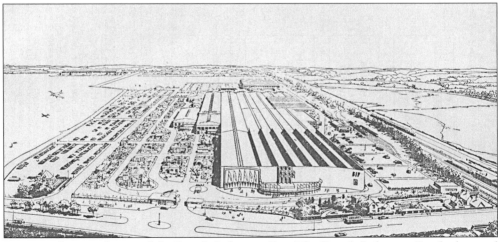

Drawing of an aerial view of the British Industries Fair. The British Industries Fair had several royal visitors, including King George V and Queen Mary in 1928.

British Industries Fair. After the Second World War, the old corrugated hangers were used by various firms for storage. The buildings were demolished sometime in the early 1970s.

Chester Road Railway Bridge, 25 May 1933.

Castle Bromwich Railway Station, 25 September 1933. In November 1840 the Earl of Bradford informed the Railway Company that he wished a station to be built at Castle Bromwich, but in March 1841 refused to sell the necessary land, unless a promise was made that trains would not stop there on a Sunday. The company agreed and the Castle Bromwich Station was built in 1842. The building seen in the photograph was opened on 10 February 1901, replacing the older structure. In 1933 history was made, when the first diesel locomotive arrived for display at the British Industries Fair. The station closed in the 1960s and was demolished in 1975.

Castle Bromwich Railway Station and track, 18 May 1931. The station was situated on the Midland Railway line, which ran through Sutton Coldfield to Aldridge and Wolverhampton. The route between Castle Bromwich and Wolverhampton was built in two sections. The first, Wolverhampton to Walsall, opened in 1872 and the Walsall to Castle Bromwich section was opened in July 1879. The passenger service on the Walsall to Castle Bromwich section ceased on 18 January 1965, but the line is still used today for freight.

Chester Road and Railway Bridge, 15 September 1937.

Chester Road Railway Bridge, 5 September 1937.

Two
Aviation at Castle Vale

ALF. P. MAXFIELD. *Birmingham's First Flying Man.*

Flights from Sept 27ᵗʰ to Oct 2ⁿᵈ at Castle Bromwich

Golf Links. 1909.   Masonic Hall, Birmᵐ

Alfred P. Maxwell, Birmingham's first flying man and Birmingham's first flying machine on display at the Masonic Hall. Castle Bromwich saw its first aeroplane in 1909. Maxwell's first two planes never flew, although his first plane was exhibited at Olympia in April 1909. Sometime between 27 September and 7 October, Maxwell transported his third machine from Aston to the playing fields at Castle Bromwich. The plane reached the dazzling height of 50 feet in one attempt.

Castle Bromwich Airfield. It was in 1911 that the peace of the playing fields was shattered again when the famous Mr Bentfield C. Hucks (later to become Captain) demonstrated a Bleriot monoplane. Mr Hucks was to give passenger flights in this plane. *Flight*, on 11 November 1911, carried its first reference to the playing fields becoming an airfield. Negotiations between the Midland Aero Club and Birmingham Corporation were almost complete and a hanger had been erected for the planes. It was hoped that one or two prominent aviators would make their headquarters there.

The City of Birmingham chartered by the Air League, arriving at Castle Bromwich for the Air Pageant in July 1928. Eighteen passengers were carried from London and back. Soon after the start of the First World War, the War Office requisitioned Castle Bromwich airfield. On 11 May 1915, No. 5 Reserve Aeroplane Squadron was formed there. The unit became the No. 5 Training Squadron. Nine other RFC and RAF squadrons resided at the airfield during and immediately after the war. After the war Castle Bromwich saw the start of the newly formed Imperial Airways home service from London. In 1922 the airfield was also used for the first round of Britain King's Cup Race. In 1926 the newly formed 605 squadron gave a demonstration to over 100,000 people.

The first aircraft airmail to land in Birmingham, c. 1930. From 1-6 October 1919, the RAF flew mail and newspapers from London to Castle Bromwich during the rail strike. The surcharge was two shillings per ounce. Vickers Limited also flew their mail between London and Birmingham and then onto Sheffield during the strike. Imperial Airways were to fly the airmail in the 1930s.

No. 15 Shed, Park Lane, April 1929. After the First World War the Drainage Board was to retake control of the bulk of the land, which included a line of huts which ran across the field. The board hoped to sell the huts to Birmingham Corporation to help with the city's housing shortage. Officially called The Bungalows, the huts were the only housing in the area except for the few houses owned by the Drainage Board. The huts were quite modern for the 1920s, having a living room, three bedrooms, a toilet and electric lighting. They were used by the workers from Dunlop.

The 'Harrow', an early twin-engine heavy bomber at Castle Bromwich. The British Industries Fair is in the background. The reoccupation of the land by the Drainage Board enabled the Parks Department to take up the use of the playing fields again. The reduced site of thirteen acres was used for football and the stabling of horses, until the late 1980s when the land became part of an industrial park.

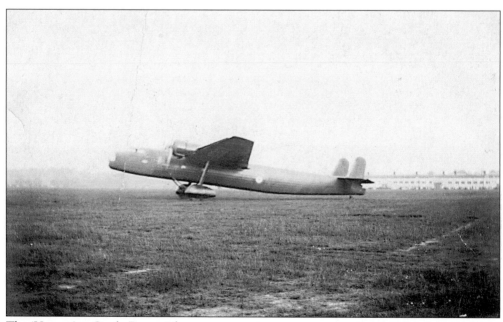

The 'Harrow' at Castle Bromwich.

The main entrance to the Nuffield factory on Kingsbury Road, c. 1943. As the inevitably of the Second World War became apparent, plans were made for the oncoming conflict. Realising the need to provide large-scale production of aircraft, the Air Minister, Sir Kingsley Wood, approached Lord Nuffield (William Morris) of the Nuffield organization with the idea of establishing a new factory. The factory was to be built between Fort Dunlop and the Castle Bromwich Airfield.

The main office and drawing office, c. 1943. On 14 July 1938, Sir Kingsley Wood, the Air Minister, cut the first sod towards the factory's construction. The Castle Bromwich factory was to be the largest of its kind in Britain; it covered some 345 acres and employed 12,000 people. The Nuffield Corporation bought the site from Birmingham Corporation and an initial order for 1,000 Spitfires was placed on 12 April 1939.

Aerial view of the Nuffield Factory, c. 1943. After being built, there was some confusion as to the production policy and it was not until June 1940 that the first Spitfire taxied from the factory to the airfield. It was at this time that the factory was placed under the control of Vicker-Armstrong and by the end of 1941 it had produced 1,298 Spitfires.

The main drawing office, c. 1943.

The Tool Room in 'F' Block, *c.* 1943.

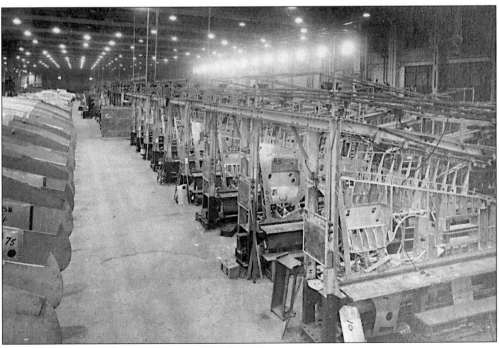

Wing Assembly for the Spitfires in 'C' block, *c.* 1943.

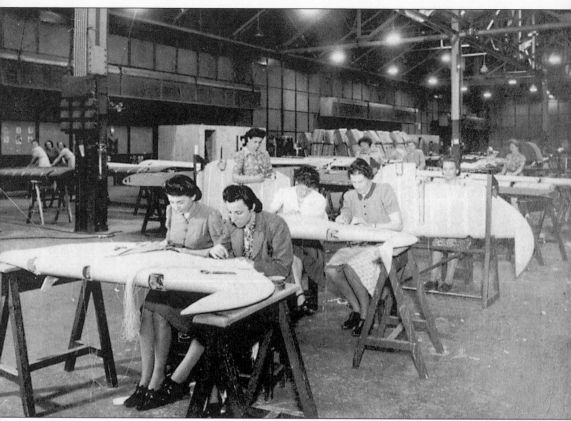

Tailplane and fin fabric covering, c. 1943. Without the aid of the women workers it is unlikely that the planes could have been built. Here the women are stitching the fabric on the rudders of the Spitfires. Later on in the war, the fabric was replaced by metal.

Sealing fabric covering the petrol tanks in the drape shop, *c.* 1943. In April 1943 a lone bomber from Vannes in Brittany dropped its bombs on the Spitfire factory at 11.30 p.m. Nineteen 50kg bombs fell, damaging 'F' and 'Q' blocks and damaging machinery in 'D' block. As a result of the raid, eight workers were killed, forty-one seriously injured and over a hundred mildly injured, and it prompted the decision to disperse production around the Midlands.

The finished parts store, *c.* 1943.

The Spitfire fuselage assembly, c. 1943. Wartime Castle Bromwich is remembered for its massive contribution to the Spitfire programme. The first Castle Bromwich Spitfire, P7280, was delivered to the RAF on 27 June 1940, and the first delivery to a squadron took place on 17 July 1940. Production targets reached thirty Spitfires a week.

Lancaster fuselage assembly, 'B' Block, c. 1943. In September 1941, 200 Lancaster Mk.11 bombers were ordered. The first of these bombers was tested on 22 October 1943. The factory was also commissioned to build fifty Seafire 45s.

A Spitfire on the runway at Castle Bromwich, 1944. During 1942 Castle Bromwich was turning out around 50 Spitfires a week. In all, more than 11,500 (some reports say as many as 11,939) Spitfires were built at Castle Bromwich and its associated shadow factories. This figure is more than half of the total number of Spitfires built during the war. The last Castle Bromwich Spitfire, PK 614, was test-flown on 30 November 1945.

The Lancaster HK 535 Bomber, c. 1943. In September 1941, 200 Lancaster HK 535 bombers were ordered. They were fitted with Merlin 22 engines, and the first one flew on 22 October 1943. The aeroplane shown in the photograph was issued to 463 (Royal Auxiliary Air Force.) Squadron and was lost during a raid on Lille during the night of 10-11 May 1944, when piloted by Flt Lt Scott (RAAF) based at Waddington. A total of some 305 Lancaster's had been built at Castle Bromwich by the end of the war.

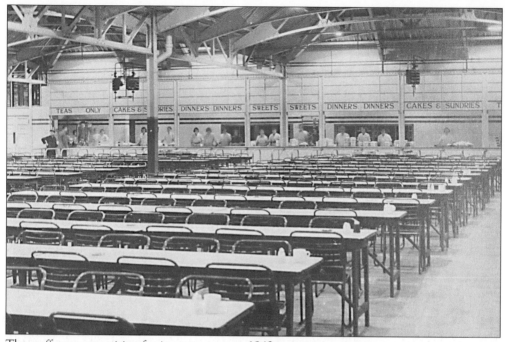

The staff canteen waiting for its customers, *c.* 1943.

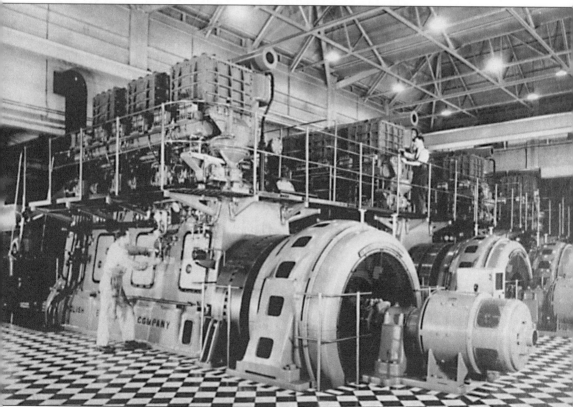

Generating plant, *c.* 1943.

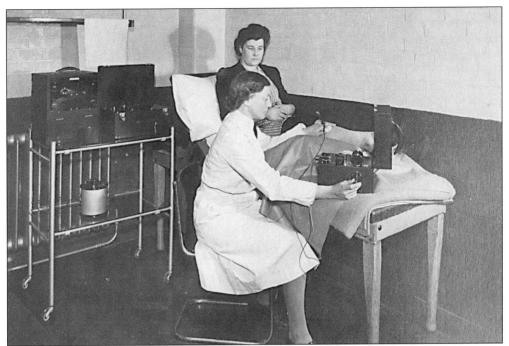

The surgery at the factory, c. 1943. During the war years there were around 311 red warnings of air raids at Castle Bromwich, lasting a total of 575 hours. More than 200 bombs were dropped on the factory and 11 people were killed.

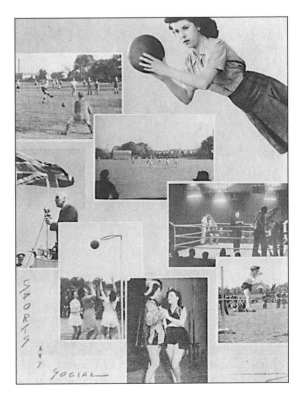

Poster advertising the Sports and Social Club, c. 1943.

Castle Bromwich Aerodrome Factory football team, 1940/41. The Castle Bromwich XI played the Allied Army XI at the Birmingham gas ground in Holly Lane, Erdington in the 1940/41 season. The goalkeeper, Harry Hibbs, played for both Birmingham and England, and was known as the 'Prince of Goalies.' This match was sanctioned by the Birmingham County Football Association to be the first ever Sunday football match. Teddy Eden of Birmingham City Football Association travelled to Lancaster Gate (the head quarters of the Football Association) to obtain verbal approval from the Football Association to permit Hibbs, and Viney the other professional footballer, to play on a Sunday.

Castle Bromwich Aeroplane Factory Technical Department wartime dance at the Crown and Cushion at Perry Barr, Christmas 1940-1941. At the time the factory was still under construction, and so all the departments worked in improvised circumstances, preparing initially for the production of 1,000 pairs of Spitfire mainplanes, and ultimately to complete aircraft MKV and MKIX. (information taken from back of photograph.)

Winston Churchill and Mrs Eleanor Roosevelt's visit to the factory, 26 September 1941. Among the many famous visitors to Castle Bromwich during the war, were the American President's wife, Mrs Eleanor Roosevelt, and Winston Churchill, who came on Friday, 26 September 1941. Sir John Colville recorded a display by a Hurricane and a Spitfire in his diary: 'Their performance was so daring as to be positively frightening and we all shuddered as Henshaw, the Spitfire pilot, flew over us upside down, some 40 feet from the ground.'

The renowned Alex Henshaw, Chief Test Pilot at Castle Bromwich with the King of Norway. In 1938-1939 Alex Henshaw became a celebrated flyer when he won the King's Cup Air Race and then broke all records in a solo flight to Capetown and back. He became Chief Test Pilot at Castle Bromwich in 1940. Henshaw is the only person to have flown a Spitfire at a very low level down Broad Street and then performed a victory roll above Baskerville House. During the six years he was there, Henshaw kept the local people around Castle Bromwich entertained with some spectacular air displays, as he put the new Spitfires through their paces. While he was there Alex tested more than 10% of the aircraft produced at the factory, including the last Spitfire built at Castle Bromwich in January 1946. Alex said of the people at Castle Bromwich, 'they built it up from nothing into something great.'

One of a set of maps taken by the Luftwaffe showing an aerial view, which the pilots would have used when flying the bombing raids. The Castle Bromwich factory was an obvious target for the German bomber pilots.

Once the planes had been built they were taxied out from the factory across the main Chester Road, to be tested on the airfield.

Aerial view of the flight sheds at Castle Bromwich.

'A' Block, M Flight Shed.

MK IX Spitfires in the HN serial range on the apron outside Castle Bromwich Flight Sheds in the Spring of 1944. The factory was closed in December 1945, and the airfield reverted back to being a training station. At the end of the war, most of the factory was sold to Fisher and Ludlow Limited, which was acquired by BMC in 1953; it was later to become part of the Jaguar works. Part of the site was bought by Dunlop who used it for their research programme.

Aerial view of the Castle Bromwich Airfield. The airfield itself closed in 1958. On 1 April a final toast was drunk in the officers mess and the airfield was closed down as a flying centre. Final closure came on 21 September 1960 when the land was sold to Birmingham City Council. The land began to be developed for the new Castle Vale Estate in May 1964.

These three aerial photographs were taken for the inquiry in March 1960 when Sutton Coldfield Corporation, acting on behalf of Warwickshire County Council, refused to grant planning permission to Birmingham City Council, who had applied to develop part of the Castle Bromwich Airfield which lay in Sutton Coldfield, for housing.

Aerial view showing Chester Road and part of the Castle Bromwich Airfield, 1960.

Three
Pre-war Castle Vale

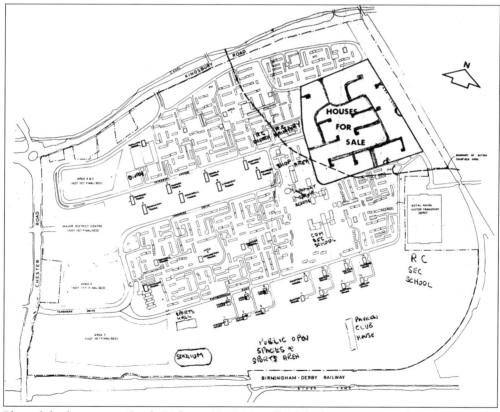

Plan of the housing at Castle Vale, *c*. 1966. Not all of the housing at Castle Vale was to be council owned. Birmingham City Council also planed to build 450 semi-detached houses and flats ranging in price from £2,474 to £3,125.

The area before the Castle Vale Development. After the war, Birmingham concentrated on its plans for rebuilding houses in and around the city. Many new estates were built in the 1930s, including the Pype Hayes Estate. As the city spread outwards, people became increasingly concerned for the Green Belt areas and ideas for 'overspill' or satellite new towns were becoming increasingly popular.

The old aircraft hangers, 1967. The purchase of the airfield by Birmingham City Council gave the Corporation its first opportunity for over a decade to demonstrate what it could do with a really large area. Castle Vale was to become the first new large-scale redevelopment for Birmingham.

Near the old aircraft hangers, 22 August 1974. The site chosen for the redevelopment presented huge constructional problems, and because it was totally flat and treeless, it contrasted with other estates rich in landscape features. After heated discussions one of two plans was decided upon.

Near the old aircraft hangers, 29 October 1975. The second plan, the larger of the 2 submitted, won. The plan of housing for 22,000 people, with 5,000 dwellings and 34 tower blocks, mostly in 2 spines down the length of the estate, was started in 1964.

Site of the former British Industries Fair. This photograph shows the view from the rear of the estate looking towards the adjacent residential development.

Looking towards Castle Bromwich, 29 October 1975. The name Castle Vale originated as a result of a newspaper competition. The word Castle being taken from the ancient motte and bailey mound (the Pimple) just up the road at Castle Bromwich, and Vale being the valley in which the area is situated.

Mr Malin and Mr Healey, starting on the back garden, 1967. Road names such as Round Moor, Long Close, Rough Coppice, Orchard Meadow and Brook Grove were early field names. Most of the roads, however, were named after aeroplanes, airfields or people who were involved with the construction of the estate.

Flats being built, 14 July 1967. Built between 1964 and 1969, the estate was originally established to house families displaced by the city's clearance programme. Early in the life of the newly-built flats they were already developing structural faults.

The site of the new Castle Vale swimming baths. The first sod being cut, 21 April 1978.

Aerial view of Castle Vale, 6 April 1969.

Castle Vale Library, September 1970. The style is typical of the 1970s.

Trade Winds, Reed Square.

The Petrol Station and Library on Turnhouse Road.

The Albatross public house, on Turnhouse Road, after demolition.

The old aircraft hanger being demolished and the new Betterware site being developed. The large redbrick hangers, constructed during the war, were used for a while for the storing of shell cases, gas masks and tyres. During the 1980s they were used to store part of the grain mountain for the European Market. After lying unused for several years, the hangers and site was purchased by Betterware in 1992. The hangers were demolished to make way for the new industrial site. The new Betterware site covers some 8.5 acres, with 140,000 square feet of warehousing and 25,000 square feet of offices and an International Distribution Centre. It was opened by John Major.

Open space and play area on Castle Vale, 2 July 1970. In 1993 tenants on Castle Vale were asked to vote on whether to stay under the control of Birmingham City Council or to opt for a multi-million pound deal with the Government and Birmingham City Council to become a Housing Action Trust. The latter would lead to the improvement of the Castle Vale area. In March 1993 the tenants voted overwhelmingly in favour of setting up a Housing Action Trust. The HAT, as it is called, was set up with the task of undertaking the complete regeneration of the Castle Vale Estate and the reversal of nearly thirty years of physical, social and economic decline.

Concrete and trees, Castle Vale, 2 July 1970. The scheme involved building fifty-seven new flats and houses on two sites, and signalled the start of the £270 million regeneration programme. Twenty-two flats were built on the site of the Albatross Public House and thirty-five houses on the land opposite. In June 1994 the HAT decided to demolish eight of the eyesore tower blocks. Residents had long campaigned for the 'centre eight,' Abingdon, Bovingdon, Cosford, Canwell, Kemble, Lyneham, Northolt and Shawbury, to be demolished. Plans drawn up by urban designer, Hunt Thompson with the help of the residents, included tree-lined boulevards, a central park and traffic calming measures.

One of the children's play areas, known as The Fort. The original ten-year plan proposes to demolish seventeen of the thirty-four tower blocks and redevelop existing homes and the shopping centre. In fact the new Sainsburys opened on 29 July 2000. Grants and private investment, including a multi-million pound grant from Central Government are funding the whole project.

Castle Vale open spaces, 2 July 1970.

Saint Gerard's Roman Catholic Junior and Infant School.

Queens Visit to Castle Vale, 30 October 1998. During her first visit to Birmingham for three years, the Queen and the Duke of Edinburgh toured Castle Vale, visiting the local radio station, Saint Cuthbert's church and meeting the Castle Vale Housing Action Trust staff at the Tunhouse Community Hall.

Aerial view of Castle Vale. An extract taken from the Castle Vale Housing Action Trust Newsletter, 1999-2000 reads, 'Six years on the results are impressive, particularly since the HAT has, from the very start, recognised that whilst the improvement of the home is vital, improving the physical fabric alone won't solve all of the problems. Jobs, training, better health, leisure, improved shopping facilities, transport and a greener, cleaner environment, together with a reduction in crime and neighbourhood nuisance, are being addressed to secure a lasting improvement... that's what 10,000 residents want and the HAT is making it happen by working with the community to make a new Castle Vale.'

Four

Castle Bromwich Hall and Church

Castle Bromwich Hall photographed for the Warwickshire Photographic Survey on 12 September 1891.

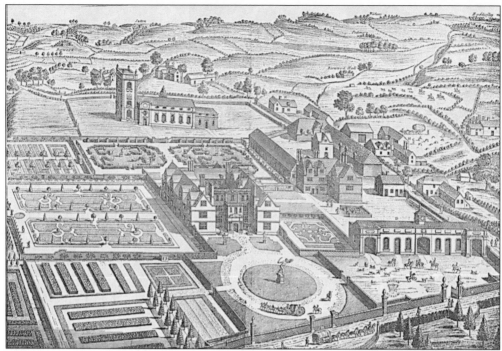

The south prospect of the Hall. At the time of the engraving the Hall was the residence of Sir John Bridgeman, having been acquired by the Bridgeman family in 1657.

The Hall as it looked in 1829. It was originally built for Sir Edward Devereux, the first MP for Tamworth in Staffordshire, towards the end of the seventeenth century. To begin with it only had a single storey. Later on Sir John Bridgeman added a second storey and built the grand entrance doorway.

The Hall was a favourite subject for nineteenth-century engravers.

A modern view of the Hall. Although owned by the Bridgeman family for centuries, the Hall was let at various times to a succession of Birmingham industrialists. The following advertisement appeared in *Aris's Birmingham Gazette* on 8 March 1773, 'to let, ready furnished, the Capitol Mansion House of Sir John Bridgeman at Castle Bromwich'.

The Hall as it was in 1891, showing the laundry.

The impressive entrance to the Hall. The Bridgemans in the eighteenth century married into the Bradford family and became Earls of Bradford. They later moved to Weston Park.

The drawing room.

The Hall in 1868. The last private resident at the Hall was Lady Ida who lived there until her death in 1936. The Hall passed through various guises and is now owned by Bovis Homes who use it as their head office for their central region. It is not open to the public.

A view of the Hall and gardens in 1868. The magazine *Country Life* featured the Hall in its issue of 17 August 1912 with some very impressive photographs.

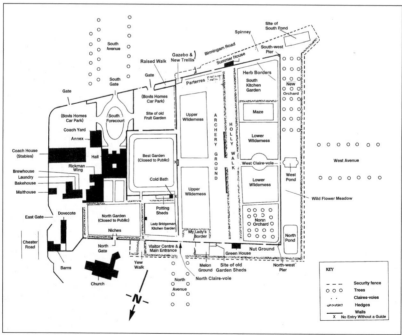

A plan of the gardens to Castle Bromwich Hall. The gardens cover over ten acres and are the only surviving example of a formal eighteenth-century garden in this country. The gardens owed their origin to Mary, wife of Sir John Bridgeman, who commissioned the landscape gardener Capt. William Winde to turn the Hall's woods and fields into a formal garden.

The entrance to the Yew Walk and the Walk itself. The walks allowed servants at the Hall to move around the gardens without disturbing the residents or their guests.

Lady Ida Bridgeman wrote of the gardens in 1898, 'I see it day by day and know every inch of and love every yard of it with my heart. It is divided into ten parts by hedges of yew, holly, box, privet and hornbeam. It is surrounded entirely by red brick walls which are almost covered by flowering creepers of every sort and kind'.

The East Orangery photographed for an article on the gardens in *Country Life* on 4 August 1900.

The Garden Steps, 1900. As the magazine wrote, 'The sweetness and radiance of flower life are, of course, here in abundance and the effects are very charming'.

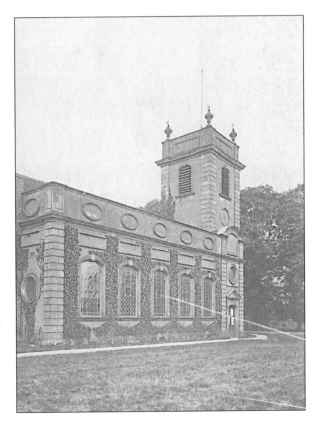

The church of St Mary and St Margaret next to the Hall, June 1891. It was originally the chapel to the Hall and only became a parish church in 1878. A rear gate leads to the Hall. The photograph was taken for the Warwickshire Photographic Survey by Edwin Middleton.

The present church was built by Sir John Bridgeman in the English Renaissance style. It was finished in 1731. He built the church around an existing fifteenth-century timber framed church, encasing the earlier building.

The chancel and old pews.

The ivy-clad exterior of the church of St Mary and St Margaret.

An interior views of the church in the 1890s. The living at that time was in the gift of the Earl of Bradford.

Epitaph to Sir John Bridgeman (1752), and the window dedicated to the memory of the Countess of Bradford who died in 1842.

The rare three-tiered pulpit and a reading desk.

Five
Castle Bromwich Miscellany

The Tumulus. Opposite the church is Castle Hill, a local landmark more recently known as Pimple Hill. The exact origins of the Tumulus are unknown but it certainly points to centuries of fortification at Castle Bromwich. It is probable that the mound was used by the Romans to guard the crossing over the River Tame below. A pattern of ditches and banks were uncovered by archaeologists in recent years, as well as evidence of a Norman castle. Undoubtedly the mound would have made a fine watchtower for any group.

The Tumulus in 1934.

Whateley Hall photographed by Sir Benjamin Stone in 1900. The house was probably built in the eighteenth century in classical style. It was situated close to Whateley Green.

The house was surrounded by considerable wooded grounds and was the second largest house in the area after Castle Bromwich Hall.

The back view of the house. It is probable that the house was built on the site of an earlier moated building.

The impressive entrance hall photographed in 1900.

The Knight family took up residence at Whateley Hall in the 1860s and remained there until 1935. The house was demolished shortly after the family left. This photograph is of the christening party for one of the Knights on 1 August 1906.

The Lodge to Whateley Hall which still exists to the left of Whateley Green, where Water Orton Lane meets Green Lane.

Whateley Green. The Green was the site of the village's stray animal pounds and of a whipping post. The smithy was also situated there. The name 'Whateley' derives from the Anglo-Saxon word for 'wheatfield clearing'.

Park Hall. Once the seat of the Arden family, this wonderful seventeenth-century mansion on the fringes of Castle Bromwich by the banks of the River Tame has long since been demolished in the name of progress.

The Hall and its surrounds, photographed by J.H. Pickard. The introduction to this book quotes the local antiquarian Thomas Chattock talking of the virtues of the area. Chattock lived at the Hall at the beginning of the nineteenth century at a time when it was entirely surrounded by woodland. This photograph, taken a century later, gives some impression of Park Hall's rural setting.

A later photograph of the Hall when it had been lying abandoned for years. The Hall had come into the possession of the Bridgeman family at the beginning of the eighteenth century. There had been an earlier house on the site as shown by a Hall and large estate being mentioned in documents dating back to 1265.

Park Hill farm bridge in the early 1930s. The Hall and estate included numerous outbuildings. Among these were a farmhouse, granary, stables, cowsheds and walled gardens, which have given way to modern housing and the M6 motorway. The name is only recalled in Park Hill School, the name of the local secondary school which is built at the top of the hill looking down to the site of the Hall.

A series of photographs of Castle Bromwich flour mill, taken by the celebrated local photographer Sir Benjamin Stone in 1894.

This mill was one of many in the area drawing on water from the River Tame, but was one of the few left still grinding corn at this date, 1894.

Castle Bromwich mill stood on the southern bank of the Tame near what is now The Firs estate.

An artist latterly used the building as a studio until it was pulled down in the 1960s.

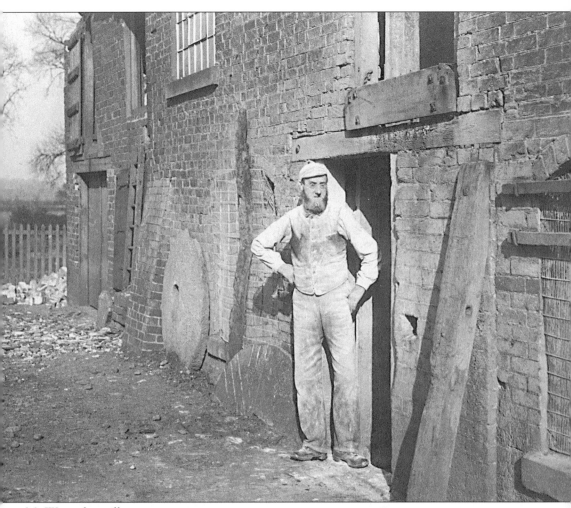

Mr West, the miller.

'The Firs' was the home of the Bosworth family in 1894 with Mr Bosworth, his wife and daughter. The post-war housing estate built on the site has taken the old name. The house was usually occupied by the estate bailiff to Castle Bromwich Hall.

The farmyard to 'The Firs'.

The entrance to Castle Bromwich village, 1899. The road to the left on the photograph leads to the parish church.

The Common to the house of Mr France in the winter of 1893.

The top of Castle Bromwich hill, 1934.

Old farm houses. Until quite recently Castle Bromwich was a distinctly rural area and a number of farmhouses and cottages have survived the redevelopment of the district.

The toll house. The Chester Road which runs through Castle Bromwich is an old Roman way and was for centuries an important highway. The road was turnpiked from 1759 until 1877 when the trust which managed it went out of business.

A very rural scene, Coleshill Road in 1923.

The Bradford Arms, one of the four old inns in Castle Bromwich in the eighteenth century. The others were the Castle Inn, the Coach and Horses and the Bridgeman Arms. Built on the site of an earlier pub – the White Lion – the inn took its present name when a rival closed in 1818.

The Bradford Arms was an old coaching inn which had at one time twenty-eight beds for long distance travellers and is Castle Bromwich's oldest pub, though now greatly extended.

A modern view of the Bradford Arms taken for the Shard End Camera Club in 1983.

Another of the four old inns, the Coach and Horses and is the only one to remain open all day. Like the Bradford Arms it was built as a coaching inn and the original building stood where the front drive of the modern pub is. The inn is mentioned in the records of the Bradford estate in 1776. Post chaises could be hired and a stableman was employed. The original building was replaced by a mock Tudor style inn around 1920 which itself was replaced after the thatched roof caught fire in 1938.

The bridge over the Tame on the Chester Road, January 1928.

The well-known roundabout at the Clock Garage. The garage marked the city boundary and was the terminus for the Birmingham buses from the city centre. For many years only the Midland Red buses would cross the city boundary up the Bradford Road to Castle Bromwich.

A fascinating aerial view of the whole area covered by this photographic collection. Castle Vale can be seen in the bottom left hand corner, Castle Bromwich in the top left hand corner and Shard End is just visible at the top on the right. The tower blocks are the Firs estate and the photograph predates the construction of the M6 and the collector road.

Six
Rural Shard End

Cole Hall farm photographed by the Shard End Camera Club in 1983.

Abraham Thornton

Shard End's most famous or infamous resident, Abraham Thornton. The son of the owner of Shard End farm, Abraham Thornton, was charged with the murder of a local girl, Mary Ashford, in 1817. The circumstances of Mary's death and the subsequent trial of Thornton are still today, nearly two centuries later, subjects of speculation and interest. The events of the trial led to the abolition in English law of two ancient rights – the right of a close relative of the victim to demand another trial even though the defendant had been acquitted; and the right of the defendant to defend himself by challenging the relative to a duel. Mary's brother, William Ashford invoked the ancient law called Appeal of Murder at the original trial at Warwick, and Thornton claimed the Right to Battle at his second trial at Westminster Hall in London on 17 November 1817.

The Thornton farmhouse in Shard End from where Abraham set out on the night of Mary's death, 25 May 1817.

A contemporary engraving of Mary Ashford.

Mary in the clothes she wore that fateful night. In all the illustrations of Mary produced after her death, the emphasis was on her innocence and youth.

MAP OF THE ROADS, NEAR TO THE SPOT
Where Mary Ashford was Murdered.

FOR the sake of perspicuity, those fields only are marked upon the map which are near to the scene of the Murder, and a few of the roads are in part omitted, where it was thought that they would tend rather to confuse than add to the utility of the map.

It may perhaps assist the inspector of the Map, to be reminded of some of the particulars of this most interesting case. The dance at which Thornton first saw Mary Ashford was at Tyburn house, which is situated on the right-hand side of the map, this was on the evening of the 26th of May, they left this place in company with Hannah Cox, about midnight, and walked together along the London and Chester road, as far as the house marked on the map, called the "Old Cuckoo," there Hannah Cox left them and proceeded to the house of her mother-in-law, Mrs. Butler, at Erdington.

Thornton and Mary were next seen at three in the morning, by Hompidge, they were sitting on the stile marked A, at the top of the Foredrough*, in Bell Lane. This Foredrough leads to a foot-path which passes through the fields, and then joins Penn's Mill Lane, which is the road to Langley, where Mary resided with her Uncle. Here it is supposed that they parted, as Mary was seen walking down Bell Lane by herself; Aspinee saw her passing by the Horse pit, as he crossed Bell Lane at Greensall's; from this spot looking northwards, it is possible to see along the lane considerably more than a quarter of a mile, as it is both wide and straight; and Mary was the only person that was seen: at four she reached Mrs. Butler's, where she changed her clothes and conversed with her friend Hannah Cox as usual. In returning from Mrs. Butler's, she was seen by three persons; Chesterton saw her come out of Mrs. Butler's entry, and turn up Bell Lane, at ten minutes after four; Dawson saw her and spoke to her between Mrs. Butler's and Greensall's; Broadhurst saw her about the place where Bell Lane crosses the Chester road: here she passed a second time by her Grandfather's, and of course would turn down the Foredrough and go through the fields, that being the shortest way. Near to the gate at which the foot-path enters the Harrowed field it has been supposed that the Murderer waited, and that probably he hid himself behind the hedge. The reader will now direct his attention to the map of the fields upon the enlarged scale; in the Harrowed field he will see the mark of the feet, sometimes running, then dodging. In the fatal field are seen the tree, the double foot-path, the track of the blood, the foot mark, and the pit; returning to the Harrowed field the reader will be able to trace the footsteps of the supposed Murderer, running first in a direction parallel with the lane, then turning suddenly and proceeding in a straight line towards the gate at the bottom of the field; from this place footsteps of a man running have been traced at intervals through the inclosures, till they reach

*This term is certain a Provincialism of Warwickshire. It means a road leaked to as both sides and landed to as inclosure.

the Chester road passing by Pipe Hall. Other footsteps, in the direction marked upon the Map, have been discovered leading to the top of the lane which passes on to the bridge; passing over this a person might reach Holden's by the towing-path, and so on down the lane and through the fields to Twamley's Mill, which is seen near to Castle Bromwich church, on the right of the map.

Thornton, in his defence, says, that Le walked with Mary Ashford from the stile marked A, down Bell Lane, to Mrs. Butler's; waited for her about five minutes, on the green marked B, but finding that she did not come out, he proceeded homewards, by means of the road marked upon the map leading towards Holden's.

Two witnesses for Thornton deposed that they saw him coming down the lane from the bridge and going towards Holden's and that this was as nearly as they could judge, about half-past Four. The opinion of the time was confirmed by a third witness. Another witness deposed that he saw Thornton coming towards Twamley's Mill as though from Erdington, at about five minutes past Five. This testimony was confirmed by one who saw Thornton there with the witness near the time sworn to. Another witness saw Thornton in Castle Bromwich about twenty-five minutes past Five. Two witnesses for the prosecution proved the deceased to have left Mrs. Butler's about ten minutes past Four. Another saw her near to Freeman's, at about twenty minutes past Four. The body was found about half-past Six, as appears by two witnesses.

In the section of the pit is seen the exact slope and height of the bank, the depth of the water, the situation of the foot-mark, and the position of the body when found: the height of the water as here represented, is as near as possible to what it was when the Murder took place.

The Vignette is a view of the pit, taken from the opposite side to that on which the body was thrown in. About the centre of the picture is seen the situation of the foot-mark, and a little to the left the stile which connects the Harrowed and the Fatal field.

DISTANCES.

	M.	F.	P.
The distance from Mrs. Butler's to the Pit, allowing for the Bending of the Roads	1	2	22
From the Pit to Holden's, following the Track	2	1	9
From Holden's to the Flood-gates of Twamley's Mill, allowing for those Turns only, which are unavoidable	0	7	166

PRINTED BY JAMES BELCHER AND SON, HIGH-STREET, BIRMINGHAM.—PRICE ONE SHILLING.

MAP of the principal Fields and Roads &c. surrounding the Pit where MARY ASHFORD was found Murdered on the Morning of the 27th of May 1817.

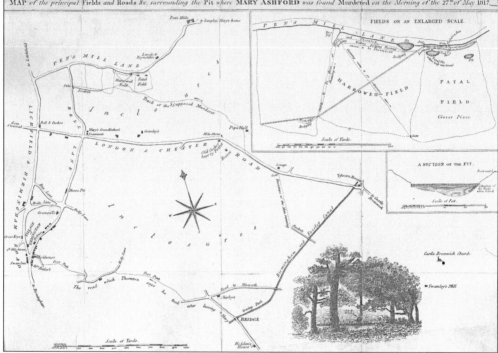

This map indicates the rural nature of the whole area pitted with footpaths and virtually no roads. The distances Mary had walked that day were considerable by today's standards. She had walked to and from the city centre, spent all day on her feet selling farm produce at the Bull Ring market and then spent the evening dancing.

102

Contemporary interest in the case was immense, with the majority of local public opinion ranged against Thornton. This publication was a rarity, arguing for his innocence. The truth of what happened that night will probably never be established but the probability is that Mary died from natural causes.

OBSERVATIONS

UPON THE CASE OF

ABRAHAM THORNTON,

WHO WAS

TRIED AT WARWICK, AUGUST 8, 1817,

FOR THE MURDER OF

MARY ASHFORD:

SHEWING THE

DANGER OF PRESSING PRESUMPTIVE EVIDENCE TOO FAR,

TOGETHER WITH

THE ONLY TRUE AND AUTHENTIC ACCOUNT YET PUBLISHED
OF THE EVIDENCE GIVEN AT THE TRIAL, THE
EXAMINATION OF THE PRISONER, &c.

AND

A CORRECT PLAN OF THE LOCUS IN QUO.

SECOND EDITION.

BY EDWARD HOLROYD,

OF GRAY'S INN.

" Judging is, as it were, balancing an account, and determining on which
" side the odds lie. If, therefore, either be huddled up in haste, and several
" of the sums, that should have gone into the account be overlooked, and left
" out, this precipitancy causes as wrong a judgment, as if it were a perfect igno-
" rance. To check this precipitancy, our understanding and reason were given
" us, if we will make a right use of it, to search, and see, and then judge
" thereupon."—LOCKE.

LONDON:

PRINTED FOR J. MAWMAN, 39, LUDGATE STREET.
1819.

The 'Tyburn House', the venue of the dance where Mary and Abraham met on the fateful night and from which they embarked on a walk to her lodgings in Erdington. The pub was commonly known at the time as the 'Three Tuns'.

The site where Mary's body was found, the so-called Mary Ashford pit, off Penns Lane, photographed in 1901.

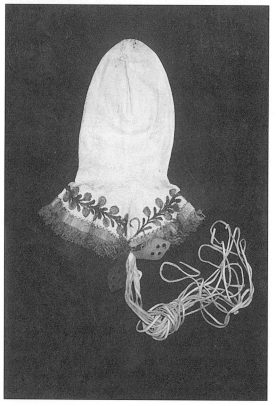

A recent photograph of the gauntlet which Abraham Thornton threw down at his trial, challenging Mary's younger brother to a duel to prove his innocence. The offer from Thornton, a burly fellow according to contemporary accounts, was turned down by the lawyer for the Ashfords, remarking that it did not serve the cause of justice for the brother to be killed as well. There had not been a Wager of Battle in England since 1638. Thornton himself eventually left the area for America and despite the best endeavours of historians since, nothing has been found out about his life there.

A

Very Desirable and Important Farm,

known as

"SHARD END FARM,"

comprising a

Good Substantial Brick and Tile Farmhouse,

Compact and Well-arranged Farm Buildings,

together with

159a. 1r. 37p.

of Arable and Pasture Land, well-watered Meadows and Woodland,

and

A Pair of Modern Brick and Tile Cottages,
with Gardens.

The Farmhouse contains Porch and Entrance, Sitting Room, Dining Room with china cupboard, Kitchen, Dairy, Larder, Scullery, two Cellars, four good Bedrooms, Dressing Room, and four Attics. Outside is a useful Covered Way leading to Paved Yard with well and pump, Bakehouse, two privies, Motor House, Cottage or Groom's Quarters used as General Stores), Fowlhouse, two Pigsties.

On the west side of House is a gravelled drive, leading direct to Pastures, and adjoining is Lawn, Shrubberies, well-kept and tastefully-laid-out Kitchen Garden, and Orchard.

The Farm Buildings, approached direct from road through covered Wagon Way into Stable Yard, comprise Harness Room and Corn Stores with Tool Stores over, three-stall Stable with loft over, two-bay Barn with floor over part and driftway, two-bay Wagon and Implement Shed opening into road, Chaff and Mixing House with Fodder Stores over, three-horse Stable, Root House, Covered Way to Rickyard, large Cattle Feeding Shed, Passage leading to Foldyard, around which are two-stall Nag Stable and Loose Box, 2-tie Cowhouse, Calf Pen, 12-tie Cowhouse, Fodder Space and Feeding Way.

There is also a good Rickyard.

The two well-built Cottages on O.S. No. 339, each contain Sitting Room, Kitchen, Larder, Coals, three Bedrooms one on Ground Floor, Paved Yard with privy, Wash-house used jointly, and there is a good water supply.

Nos. 343, 318, 320 and 325 are in hand, and the remainder is let to Mr. William Wood at a rent of

£173 0s. 0d. per annum.

A bill advertising the sale of Shard End farm in 1919. The farm was part of the Coleshill estate.

Two views of Cole Hall farm. The recollections of an old resident, Frank Wilkinson, gives a picture of a different world. He remembers, 'Mr Edwards's farm was at the corner of Shustoke Road and Shard End Crescent. A duck pond was on the other side of the road where there are now bungalows. Nearby was another farm run by Mr Adams. I worked there for two weeks but it was not my cup of tea so I left. Mr Mitchell was the farmer then in 1924'.

Old farm cottages in Shard End. Difficult as it is to imagine for those who know the area today, right up to the end of the Second World War, Shard End was completely rural with the only buildings being farmhouses, tithe cottages and farm outbuildings.

Mr Mitchell, or 'Squire Mitchell' as he was known locally, posing for the camera in the late 1920s.

Open spaces waiting to be built on. The remains of buildings shown here have come from the Midland sand and gravel company who operated a mine in the inter-war period. During the Second World War the gravel pit was used to store and repair third-line tanks. The site was landscaped after the war and is now part of the Norman Chamberlain Playing Fields.

The site of the entrance to the proposed playing fields opposite Shard End Crescent, October 1956.

The view looking north towards Packington Avenue.

A general view of the new estate looking south-east.

North-west view, February 1958. The estate was added to in stages, producing some variety in the housing.

Scouting

The Official Organ of the Birmingham & District Association of Boy Scouts

CONTENTS

Vol. 1   JUNE, 1920   No 9

Price TWO-PENCE

Yorkswood on the fringes of Shard End became the site of a permanent scout camp, built and owned by the Birmingham Association of Boy Scouts. Much of the actual woodland had been cut down to help the war effort and consequently the scouts were able to buy the land at a bargain rate.

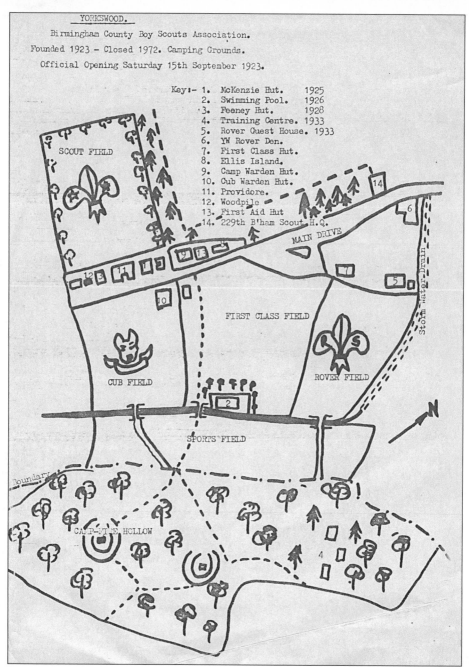

A plan of the camp. The scouts were pleased with their acquisition of the woods. Writing in the *Scouting* magazine the editor reported on his tour of the site under the headline 'Yorkswood Camp De Luxe'. He enthused, 'seriously this new camp site of ours is absolutely the goods, and the above title is not at all exaggerated, for before we go any further the permanent wash-houses and latrines are a great boon in themselves… As far as the ground is concerned we could have done a great deal worse. There are five splendid fields, so there will be one each for Cubs, Rovers, Scouts, Cofton and a recreation field. These cover an area of twenty five acres'. In all the site covered over two hundred acres.

112

The entrance to the camp and the training centre. The *Scouter* also reported on the nearby river and brook which was said to be providing water which is 'sweet, clean and deliciously cool'. Moreover 'it is not necessary to take an iron cow to camp, for fresh milk may be procured daily from the Cock Sparrow Farm, about one hundred yards from the camp, if one attends at the right time of day'.

A typical camp. The Camp Fire Hollow was created in 1930 with eight tiers and a stage in the centre.

The entrance to the camp was flanked by a series of statues of griffins which after the closure of the camp were placed on the housing estate built on the site of the camp. The griffins had been taken to the camp from the city centre department store 'Lewis's when the store was being renovated. Up until then they had formed part of the decoration on the roof top gardens at Lewis's.

The future of the griffins is currently the subject of a local debate as to whether they should be returned to the city centre.

Seven

Shard End Estate

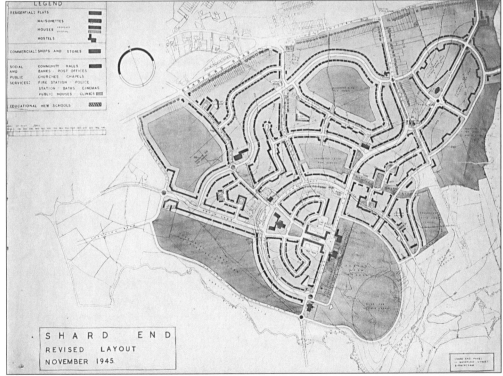

A plan of the new Shard End housing estate, November 1945. Compulsory Purchase Orders were served on the owners of the land which became Shard End estate on 12 April 1946. The schedules for the Orders indicated just how few buildings were on the land at that date and therefore how attractive the land was to the city which was looking to build overspill housing. Negotiations had taken place earlier with the farmers and landowners so that the whole area was acquired by Birmingham City Council as one package.

How the plans eventually worked out. Two aerial views of the estate from 1961. The council estate proved attractive to Brummies facing the loss of their homes to redevelopment in the inner areas of the city.

The early years of the estate. Hurst Lane opposite house Nos 70-90, as pedestrians try to negotiate what passed for footpaths.

The newly built houses on Berrowside Road, December 1951.

Typical housing on the estate.

When the estate was first built there was for tenants a marked contrast in housing, compared to accommodation in the inner city areas they had left behind, and the estate was very popular. Subsequently some of the housing has deteriorated markedly.

The clean lines of Pithall Road and the police station.

Shard End pool.

Players in the Shard End carnival pose for a press photograph in 1956.

Communal facilities lagged behind the building of new houses. For many years Shard End lacked a permanent library building and library services were operated from a mobile library service. This photograph shows Mrs Lily Albutt of No. 80 Pithall Road, selecting books from Roy Downes the travelling librarian.

Shard End library.

The official opening of the library with one of the first customers. The library opened on 24 February 1967 and instantly proved popular. In its first five months, over one hundred thousand books had been lent for home reading.

The library at Shard End was the first of Birmingham's branch libraries to adopt the plastic membership cards replacing the traditional library tickets.

Shard End community centre, 1983.

The children's playground at Norman Chamberlain Playing Fields, June 1963.

Fishing in the pool in the summer of 1974.

Two views of the pool at the playing fields in 1956 and 1983. After the war when the gravel mine had been used to store tanks, the pool was constructed as a leisure facility for the estate. The pit filled with water from a natural spring and was very dangerous. The sides were deceptively steep and there were quite a few drownings. Numerous safety features have now made it safer and it is still a delightful place for fishing and other water activities.

Norman Chamberlain playing fields, with the avenue of trees leading down from Castle Bromwich Hall, 1983.

The bowling green in Pithall Road.

All Saints church in Coneyford Road. The church was opened by the Queen in November 1955. It had the distinction to be the first Church of England church anywhere in the country to be built and consecrated after the war.

The church was built on a grand scale with the patronage of Keble College in Oxford which had a trust fund to help finance Christian worship and mission in deprived districts of Birmingham. It seats over four hundred, a challenge to fill for even the most charismatic of vicars!